Tobacco Roots
Just this side of WWII

Tobacco Roots

Just this side of WWII

Connie L. Vice

Grateful Steps
Asheville, North Carolina

Grateful Steps
159 South Lexington Avenue
Asheville, North Carolina 28801

Copyright © 2013 by Connie Williams Vice

Library of Congress Control Number 2013938915

Vice, Connie Williams
Tobacco Roots,
Just this side of WWII

Illustrated by the author; cover photograph by the author

ISBN 978-1-935130-48-2 Paperback

Printed in the United States of America

FIRST EDITION

www.gratefulsteps.org

To the people of Ewing and of Fleming County,
about whom this is written,
some named, many unnamed.

Table of Contents

Author's Note

Writing about a small Kentucky community during the '60s might seem little more than a walk down memory lane. But nostalgia, while ever so pleasant, is just the bones of my poetry. Walk with me. I promise I'll put meat on those bones—for instance, the value of childhood freedom, the importance of place and community. The rhythm of time pulsating at the edge of consciousness will boom forth in the lens of retrospect.

If born to be an author, I certainly wasn't born to write. The mechanics of writing (spelling, punctuation and even verb tense) were my stumbling blocks. But the universe offered me opportunities to work though it all. One came in the form of my sixth grade teacher, Miss Donovan. She helped me see myself in a new light, giving me hope and courage to strive for the skills and knowledge I desired. By the sixth grade, I was very behind in reading. This was because the teaching methods were memorization and sounding vowels. While those were good for most, they eluded me. With my new spirit of belief and determination, I was certain there was a third way to be a good reader. I read and read until I found it. I realize now that I learned to read by following the content of stories. I could hear the story in my head and than reflect the words back onto the page. The thrill of reading fired my determination. It is my belief and experience that the universe is never flat or just two dimensional. Things don't have to be just either-or. There is always at least a third dimension to lift us above and sometimes beyond.

In high school, another teacher, Miss McKee, introduced the classics *Ivanhoe*, *Great Expectations* and *Wuthering Heights*. My sophomore English Teacher, Mrs. Collins, one day opened our text, laid its spine along her arm, steadied it at the base with her other hand and slowly strolled across the front of the room reading Frost's "Stopping by the Woods on a Snowy Evening." I was STUNNED. For a moment, the room seemed suspended, my first thought "Ah, so that is poetry." That day is long past; the joy of discovering poetry continues. There is poetry in all things that allow imagination. I don't mean just poetry of words but the poetry of living each moment.

Tobacco Roots evolved as I began giving attention to memories and allowing them to unfold. They played in my mind, not unlike a sit-com, all the moods and feelings just bouncing into each other to create a funny, crazy, mellow life of their own. The slow, humming atmosphere of Ewing, Kentucky, in the '60s set the tempo and gave leave to savoring all the subtleties and mysteries of each moment and person.

Perhaps as you share my stories you will feel your own stories start to rumble. I encourage you to apply the magic of imagination and allow the soulful abstracts of life, which go beyond mere facts, to emerge.

–Connie Williams Vice

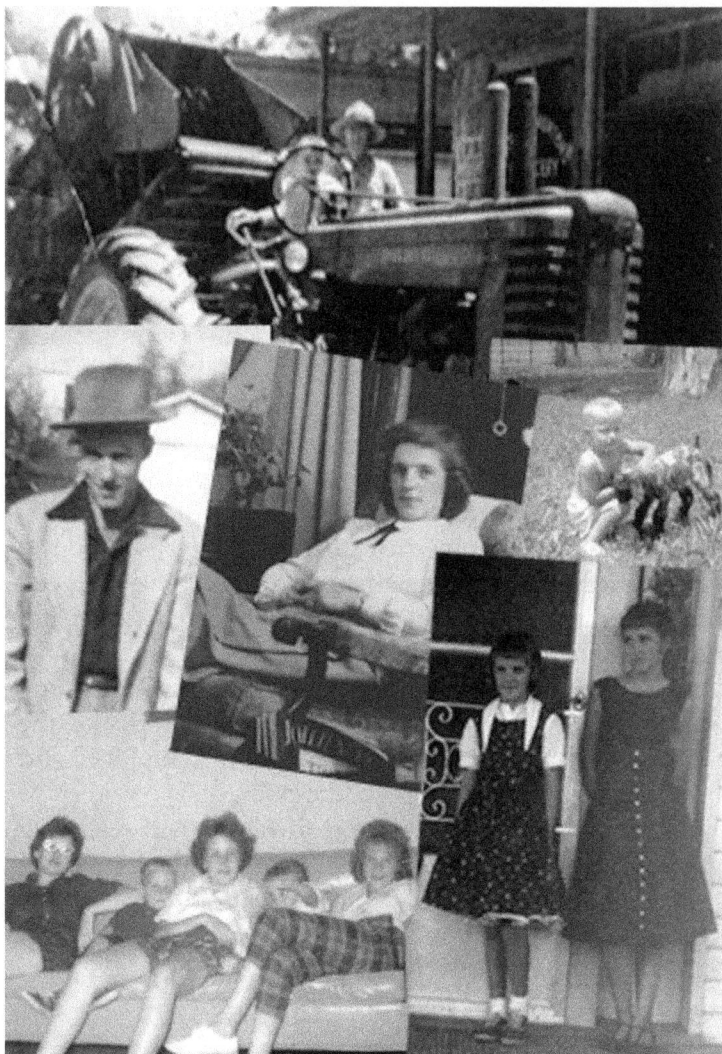

Just This Side of WWII

Growing up free and poor
I remember
not so much as a process,
but as if I float above,
watching through the blur
of clouds, waiting—
because I know from
time to time, something of
that girl, the one I was,
will grab me and zoom me
back to that life
just this side of WWII,
to my tobacco roots,
and once again
I'll feel so richly unbound.

Our Tractor Caravan

Was it a memory? No.
More vivid and from nowhere.
It was a flashback.
Simple and of no historical significance.
Not even a personal life event.
Just a brief intense vision.

It is spring, tobacco-setting time.
Our small caravan originates at Aunt Lute's.
Daddy leads on the John Deere
Bought brand new in the year of my birth.
He drives standing from time to time,
Quick and assured, his every move.

Cathie comes next on the "Little Red Tractor,"
Both hands firmly on the steering wheel,
She drives with confidence . . . she has that air.
Last in line, Patti and I,
Bare legs dangling over the wagon bed,
At ease as we bounce along.

Topping the Ewing Train Bridge,
The day warm and sunny,
As we pass Bodie's Store,
Some town "loafers" wave hello—

As our little caravan heads home,
Daddy leads, Cathie right behind
Patti and me . . .
Bare legs dangling over the side.

As a Cloud of Dust Rises up Behind

My Daddy wasn't perfect;
I've always known that.
But little it matters, he was gallant and real.

I vision him, Daddy,
Standing straight up on the green John Deere,
One arm stretched to steer.
He stands looking as if to survey.

Is it the crops, the land, the feel of the sun
That seem so pleasing to him
In that khaki ball cap
As a cloud of dust rises up behind?

Even now on a warm summer eve,
I can hear him singing "Sweet Georgia Brown"
As we work into the night—
Daddy, my sisters and I by the tractor light.

Setting tobacco into the ground,
He teased us for being sissies,
His way of saying we were tough little girls . . .
And tender too.

Frank

A simple farmer
in his work boots
walking toward me,
his never-ending smile,
his eyes dancing,
his body projecting joy.

Our neighbor Frank,
a man at peace with life.

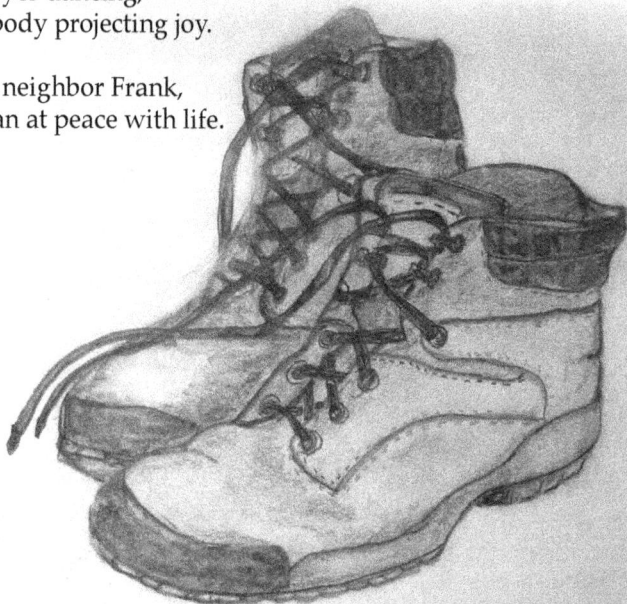

A Paradoxical Gift

I would not have chosen
To hoe a single weed in the hot sun.
I would not have chosen
To bend my pliant child body
And pull plants of tobacco for the setting.

Perhaps my father would not have
In stoic detachment
Dispensed his demands of hard work
Like a banquet to feast on,
Except for his capacity to embrace necessity.

Were it not necessary
To go to the fields in the heat of summer,
How could I have known
The happy melody of the walk home,
As the sun set and the earth cooled.

Except for necessity
Would I have grasped the demands of hard work
Discovering that which stretched me
Beyond the boundaries of potential
Into the joys of reality?

Could it be those things seeming most difficult,
Even grievous to us,
The things of necessity,
Hold some of the best gifts of the universe?
Oh, how the universe loves paradox.

Three Cedars Farm

My sister now remembers it
As Cedar Ridge Farm.
But, it was Three Cedars Farm.
I know because I recall
THREE CEDARS FARM on the mailbox
Would cause my heart to swell.

By the time my family lived there,
Only two of the cedars stood.
Perhaps that's the reason
She turned the name around.
Plus, we never spoke it,
We only said "home."

Why do I recall it so clearly—
Chipped paint on a mailbox?
The words just made me happy.

The land was not dispensable.
We lived from it, and in return,
We walked its lanes and fields.
Three Cedars Farm gave us history, place;
Wouldn't any child's heart adhere?

Cinemascope

I sit there in my watching place,
The deep windowsill of the old house,
facing east.
For a while I see the contrast:
Deep, dark-hued oranges, reds and blues.
The earth and its trees outline the lower edge
in dramatic black.

Then the light disperses—
No more drama, just muted grays.
The sky no longer excites my senses.
I will myself to *continue in it,*
and I am struck by the calmness.

Suddenly, rewarding my attention,
the sky gives me a gift. The rippled clouds
in florescent rose, pink, lavender and silver.
begin to reflect rays of the yet-to-be-seen sun.

And we thought the ancients were without cinemascope!

Worthington's Garage

We ran in a small pack, on foot.
No bikes—Mickey, Patti and me.
Often Steve,
Maybe another or two.

The hot spot was
Worthington's Garage.
It smelled of grease and sweat
And engine smoke.

Buster, the proprietor,
Had a turn toward sternness
But was too busy to pay
Us much mind.

He was always partially hidden
Behind a face shield, wheedling
His torch of blue flame to melt iron
Or lying face-up under a car.

There was a car lift
But, we weren't allowed near it
Except the few times Buster
Relented to our pleas.

And let us to take a
Seat inside a car and prop
Ourselves at a window, as he
Inched us higher and higher.

Because We Could

What a playground
We had!
The whole little town
Was ours.

All the backyards of Ewing were
At our disposal, and like little spies,
We saw and heard all there
Was to see and hear,

Making our own imaginary adventures
From all the information.
You see we had no real bother
About other peoples' business.

There were no deep or hidden
Motives or agendas to our days;
We explored the yards, the streets
And buildings just because we could.

Wasted days . . .
Ah yes,
The wonderful wastefulness
Of youth!

Lambie Pie Lost

Just a few months old and missing.
We searched the barns and the fields,
calling, "Oh Lambie Pie,
come home, little lamb of ours."
His two "mothers" pleading, praying.
Yes, two mothers, ages 8 and 9,
charged to bottle feed baby Lambie
because he had no ewe mother.

The grown-ups said, "A pack of wild dogs
are about." Oh no! Not that.
Not vicious dogs . . . and if lambs,
what of little girls?
We, the mothers, took to the house
with visions of poor Lambie and
of snarling dogs. Now helpless, we
watched from windows and hoped.

Then! Our grandfather,
who walked everywhere,
came in to say, "He's fallin' through
the cattle guard."
We ran to see, wild dogs forgotten.
There he was, poor little Lambie Pie,
down in that dugout hole,
weak and barely baaing.

"Daddy, Daddy, hurry rescue our baby lamb."
Always heroic, he yanked out
a couple crossbars and agilely reached down
and pulled Lambie Pie out,
laying him into the arms
of his waiting mothers—
who nursed him back to health
with buckets of warm milk.

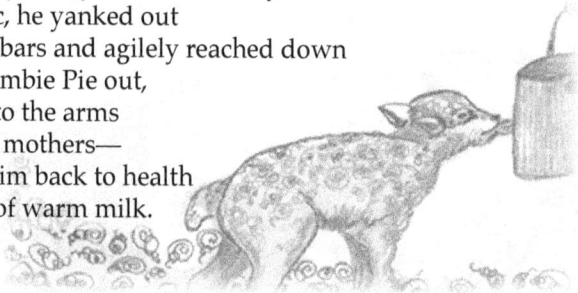

Family Ritual

The time I most loved my tobacco roots
Was the day Daddy burned the beds.
It was late March with the earth just softening,
Its fragrance all around.

I wasn't informed of the day ahead.
My parents often weren't concerned
With keeping us kids perpetually alerted
About everything.

But, I knew when I stepped from the bus
And smelled the woody smoke.
The exhilarating rush of independent discovery.
A gift from my mom and dad.

As we sisters got closer to the house,
We looked down the ridge
And saw Daddy already hard at work
Burning the tobacco beds.

In the house, Mother had a grocery sack
Of hotdogs, buns and marshmallows,
And cardboard cartons of six-ounce Cokes,
Sitting on the kitchen counter.

Changing into tight-legged, side-zipped slacks,
Pulling sweatshirts over blouses,
And slipping into pairs of old loafers,
Zoom! we were off.

The four of us shoulder to shoulder
In the pickup cab, 'cross the open field
Bouncing along in unison
Like we had a train to catch.

As dusk set in, the flames,
Like a muse, called us . . .
To share the falling of night,
The heat of consuming fire.

Our rushing there dissipated
Into just watching the tractor inch
The wire frame of fiery coals
Along beds of turned earth.

Searing steam from the furrows
As sections in sequence
Slowly lost their hot glow
To the cooling air.

Daddy
Hurled limbs on the fire,
Creating blasts of sparks that crackled
High into the dark.

Mesmerized, until hunger set in.
Then as if on cue
Each did her part to arrange the spread
Onto the banged up tailgate.

Daddy took his pocketknife
And whittled limbs into skewers,
Long ones requiring our strength
To balance dogs above the fire.

Marshmallow toasting was
about Daddy's challenge
That we brown and not char them,
As he so masterfully accomplished.

I always met that challenge,
suffering the heat even longer
In spite of the fact that I like
My marshmallows a bit charred.

Soon after that we packed up
And headed to the house.
Knowing part of the magic
Was settling back to routines.

Leaving Daddy to finish alone,
I knew he didn't mind.
He had things to ponder and plan,
A few cigarettes to smoke.

In those few hours we were baptized
By fire and night earth,
Bathed in the smoky aroma
Of our sacred family ritual.

Tobacco Roots:
Sustaining Disconnect

In me there's a sustaining disconnect
To honor my etymon
Between the perils of tobacco use
And my tobacco roots.

We didn't choose tobacco.
Some ancestor generations ago
Saw the demand, found the land,
Grew the crop, passed it on.

We raised cows, chickens and corn,
Hauled water for a fee,
But it was tobacco money
Most kept the wolves from our door.

The T-Bird Girls

Remembering,
I can actually
See, hear, feel us there,
Heading down that
Tree-lined path,
In the spring, after school.

There it sat
Quietly waiting.
Black and sleek, the dream of any boy.
It was built for two.

But we had our girlish figures
And could easily fit five.

All of us in, in a flash,
Our giggles and chatter infusing life
Into Linda's '58 T-bird.

With the turn of the key,
Its powerful engine
Joined our joyful chorus—
.
Peeling off into the small town streets,
Slightly wild,
Living for the moment.
At the top of our game.
The T-bird Girls of '65.

Evermore Turned Differently

The voice of Mr. Cronkite
Stopped me,
Caused my body to sag
With shock and grief.

He had to tell the nation
The shot that occurred
Took our leader, a hero to many,
To his death.

Unlike with Lincoln, Garfield, McKinley,
The people saw it unfold,
Witnessing hour after hour
In helpless disbelief.

We watched the slow procession,
Our president mounted
On a huge topless car
Like a knight on his steed.

Soon another procession
We attended in speechless somber,
The sidewalks fully congregated,
With weeping people, children at their sides.

The earth
Barely moved on its axis.
It would reboot,
Yet evermore turn differently.

The cog of innocence
Ripped out.
The hum of Camelot . . .
No more.

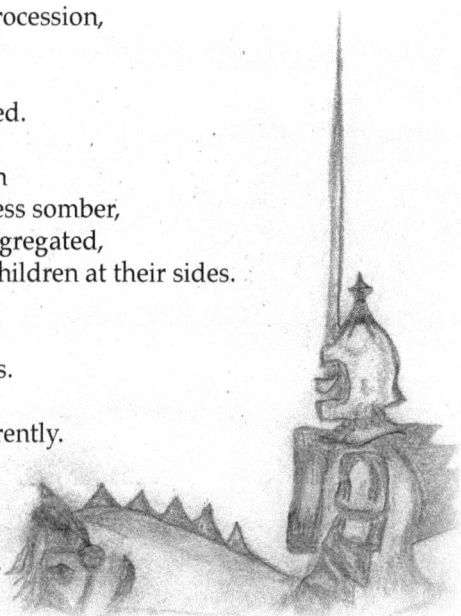

Of Roses

What of roses
moves the deepest chord in me?
What of roses
can lift me out of gloom?

The fragrance, perhaps?
The olfactory effect.
That sense of total recall,
takes me back
to the farm of my youth
so beautifully utilitarian,
except for patches of
half-kept flower beds and
the huge old rose bush
gone wild
that belonged to
my gentle, quiet grandmother.

Is it these memories?
Or simply the rose undefined.
Because, you know, nature defies
Our ability to reason or explain.
.

45 RPMs

On Saturdays we cleaned our room,
Cathie's, Patti's and mine.
A big room,
Nothing new, hodgepodge furnishings.

Good light though, thick old walls,
Two beds—double and twin.
Oldest and youngest in the double.
Mine the twin (odd man out again).

Once things were tidy,
Out came record player and 45s.

Ain't that a shame.
My tears fell like rain.
Ain't that a shame
You're th' one to blame.

I heard that song today
and went back to our room.

The sounds
Are different now:
No scratchy undertones
Or rhythm of a turntable.

My heart,
No longer 13, removed from

You said goodbye, you made me cry.

The freshness and excitement of
Adventuresome new love.

Ah! 45 RPMs
Ah! Fats.
Ah! My youth.

Tribby's Corner

We set out
In our big Mercury
After church,
Going to Tribby's Corner.

Just a tiny grocery.
Set alone
At an intersection
Of county roads.
.
We seldom went there
During the week;
On Sundays
It was the only place open.

We all went inside
And muddled about the store
As if we hadn't already
Memorized the small inventory.

I remember one Sunday
My mother
Allowed me to buy
My first pair of nylons.

I sat in the back seat
Stroking my treasure.
I chuckle now . . .
How I hate hosiery!

Soul-Singing Drowning Men

Sundays, in the freshness of our teens,
with the last syllable of the benediction,
we exploded out the closed doors
into the intense heat.

We alone occupied the Sunday sidewalk,
Just across the way
stood the Strawberry Methodist Church,
its doors wide open.

Voices of jubilee . . . *I was sinking* . . .
rocked . . . *far from the peaceful shore* . . .
right out of that tattered frame building
onto the summer street.

My body moved ever so slightly t'ward it
because, as Judy Collins once sang,
Only a drowning man can see Him.
But my mind rose up, "Don't, you aren't allowed!"

Oh! To cross over
to the Strawberry Methodist Church
with its soul-singing drowning people
seeing Him.

Ask the Stars and the Breezes

I cannot give you answers,
my child, she said.

Your own power is enough
and your fate best left to find you.

I direct you to the stars and the breezes;
Sing to them your questions of life.

Sunday Visits

Most winter Sundays after church in Ewing, Kentucky, we were at her door, my sister and I, holding our white Bibles and seeking a warm place to wait for our mother to take us home. We waited patiently after knocking because we knew she moved with a cane. Her slowness was also about her refusal to hurry.

On seeing us she motioned us in, as if we came every day. It was her way to appear complacent. She had keen observations and a witty humor. She could, in one short sentence, tote up any person or situation with clarity and wit, often making us laugh. Her summations usually edged toward kindness, but for some of her victims, not so much.

The house had four rooms—a dining room, a bedroom with a sitting area, another bedroom and a small kitchen. The kitchen was a conversion; once it was a hallway. The house had been a single dwelling, but as long as I could remember it was divided in half to make two small living spaces.

Miss Mary's half was dark, but not gloomy. We sat beside a roaring fire in the combo bedroom/sitting room—Miss Mary taking her chair, which was next to a small table with a dim lamp, we sisters taking our places facing her on the other side of the grate fireplace. There was always a fire; we only came in the winter. In the warmth of summer, we would wait for our mother on the church steps.

Each time we came she served us very cold six-ounce Cokes. And she told us intriguing stories, tales of times past. How she had four boys in World War II—one missing in action for many weeks—shaking her head as if she still couldn't believe the miracle that all four came home to her.

She told us family stories, ones no one in the family thought to tell us . . . she wasn't actually family. Some stories were about the year our father rented a room from her in Cincinnati. Renting was how she provided for eight children, not all actually hers. "Your daddy worked in a factory before going to war," she reported. "He was never cut out to punch a clock."

There was a strange closeness between her and my father. I don't even remember seeing them in the same room, but when they spoke of one another there was humor, respect and love in the undertones. I thought, What does "punch a clock" mean? I didn't ask because I understood the essence of what she said.

She was pushing 80 years old, smoked cigarettes, skillfully allowing them to hang from her lip as she talked. A small woman, she had pretty hair, which she knotted in the back, loose strains framing her face. She wore collared, cotton, dark-print dresses, with the hemline at the ankle. Her shoes were black leather, thick-heeled lace-ups. She was uniquely both old fashioned and beyond her time.

As a young adult I visited Miss Mary in the nursing home; her stories left me indebted to her—a happy liability indeed. She was beyond her 90th birthday, diabetic, sometimes lucid, sometimes not. Once, seemingly out of the blue, she asked, "Do you think God has forgotten me?" The question unraveled me; in all those Sunday visits she had never spoken of God or been philosophical, at least not straightforwardly so.

I mumbled a somewhat assured "Oh, no." She looked at me directly and seemed so lucid at that moment. I thought she was wishing herself back home in her half-house in Ewing. I now realize her query was about being left here on earth of no use to anyone. All her life she had been fiercely independent, and she had outlived several of those sons who came home to her from war. Soon after that visit God remembered her.

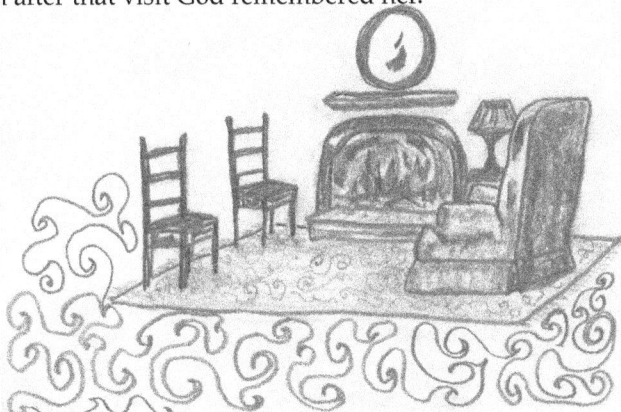

23

Seeding of Creativity

Little scavengers, we were.
Piecing together scraps of fabric
To clothe our dolls,

Using match sticks and string
To construct miniature fences—
Community planning—kid style.

A small creek needing
A bridge—not a problem
For little-girl engineers.

With a pile of loose dirt
And a pail of water,
We became architects.

A container lined with velvet:
A jewlry box.
Budding designers.

Scarcity—the seeding of creativity.

Daddy's Caddy

She had her daddy's big new Caddy
With its "push-button" windows.
Very cool and all that too back then.

Springtime in Kentucky,
Our boys, "The Panthers,"
Had donned their baseball uniforms.

A vision no red-blooded,
Teenage American girl
Would miss the sight of.

So, we loaded into the Caddy,
Cruised the town once
And headed to the game.

Down a two lane
About twenty miles,
Girls off to "cheer on" their guys.

The road straight (for Kentucky),
The music and chatter in full gear,
Windows up—the Caddy had air!

I sat in the back of that huge car,
Laughing, talking
To my heart's content.

We passed a farm truck,
And I took a second glance.
Is it not moving?

Or are we going that fast?
I leaned up to see and calmly proclaimed,
"We're going a hundred!"

The Caddy so smooth no one knew!
With just a tap on the brake,
We continued our flight to Tollsboro.

Hey, we had a mission:
Our guys had
Donned their baseball uniforms.

High Secret Places

I feel watched.
Eyes peer down.
Yes, there in the tree, my son.
Perched high in secret.

I know because of a time past,
I, too, sat high in my tree
To survey the cows, the crops,
A truck down the lane.

To become one removed, an observer.
The delight of being unseen.
Now I pretend not to see my son
So quiet, clever and serene.

I remember my grandfather
Walked beneath. I didn't breathe.
He walked right on by.
I was unfound, still free.

Next came my sister.
She called, wanting to play.
I laughed inside.
She didn't know the joy of my tree.

As my mother passed, searching for me,
I jumped from my tree.
"I'll tell you, just you
Of my high secret place."

Now I am the mother,
My son comes to share
The magic of his tree.
Our secret, our joy.

Piano Lessons

Mrs. Runyon allowed me to stand there quietly,
A kindness not many piano teachers would permit.

Even as I huddled close and intensely watched,
I never wished to play the piano.
I didn't think, *If I could be the one who gets to play . . .*
Accepting freed me to watch, to hear the mechanics.

My eyes scarcely left the keys as Janet picked out tunes.
The music in broken timing,
The resonant sound of striking keys against the hallowed walls.
Mrs. Runyon's voice or sometimes hands giving gentle
directions.

At that young age,
I knew what was real in me.

Music is not my gift.

To suck up all my surrounding,
To feel the entirety of the room—

That is my gift.

Eggs in Your Jeans Pockets

When I was 7 or 8,
Running free-as-a-buck on the farm,
Throwing caution to the wind,

I often found eggs in the hay loft,
Carrying Granny's basket.
This day finding eggs was unplanned.

Slipping them in my jeans' pockets, they fit quite well
Until . . . my leg bent, stepping down on the ladder rung.
Stopping . . . dead . . . with the first crack—too late.

I remember, tears welling up,
Messy, slimy eggs in my pockets,
And Mommy trying not to laugh as she explained:

"Honey, you can't carry eggs in your jeans pockets."

Adult Monkey Bars

I wish they made adult monkey bars.
Maybe that's what those climbing walls are about.
But, you have to cling to them.
No swinging from bar to bar, monkey style.

I remember hanging upside-down
Anchored by hinged legs from a bar.
If wearing a dress, I would be told
"Don't show your panties."

I tended to forget that and other rules of etiquette,
Especially when faced with invitations like
Watching the world inverted,
Exasperating those in charge of me.

For the joy of the moment
Can I recapture my hang-from-the-monkey-bars
Free spirit—
The one who showed her panties?

Shh . . . I Think I Hear My Voice

I love to climb, and
always intended to climb mountains.
But never have.

I painted scenes in my mind,
planning to do so with a brush.
But painted only some.

Other voices came, offering doubt.
"She can't read good."
"She must not be smart."
I knew I was smart enough!

So, please shh . . .
I'm listening to hear my own voice.
It's distant, but I hear it.
How strong could it yet be?

Wandering into the Barn

I would wander
up to the huge double doors,
pausing just a moment
then gently stepping across the shadow
into the stillness.

A massive cool cavern,
the leftover smell of cured tobacco.
On one side is a big stack of hay.
I climb to its top, lie down on my stomach.
Hands propping my chin,
I survey the place and tell myself stories.

On the other side is my dad's workbench.
Touching a wrench or smelling the grease,
I grasp
the satisfaction he contrived from that workplace.
I stoop to inspect under the bench
things forgotten and broken—all wrapped in spiderwebs.

Eventually I find the absolute center of that barn
and sit right down in the dirt, Indian style, facing the back doors.
The brilliant sun creates a kaleidoscope of light
exposing veils of dust particles that twirl and dance to my delight.

I was a wanderer, maybe even a loner.
The times allowed it—
being gone for hours, of no one's concern.
A smell, a place of cool relief, a shadow
might unexpectedly transport me back
to briefly encounter bliss.

Practice

Not only did I master monkey bars,
but, with my sister and friends,
I learned to tight-wire walk
on wooden fences.

No mother or father inching along
the side to catch or protect us.
No such distraction.

Self-taught, we did fall time after time,
using that innate childhood
ability to land.
Eventually we could walk
forever on wooden fences.

Another summer we devoted
to walking on stilts.
The town boys got them.
Whenever we girls came to town,
they, being ever so manly,
taught us the skill.

By August we could stilt walk
the two flights of stairs outside
the Ewing Baptist Church,
no parents watching.

We could also take those stilts
in wide running strides down the sidewalks.
Losing balance was nothing—
just lean into it and land on your feet.

Those summers we were
free to practice balance, focus,
resilience, independence, camaraderie and
not least of all, adventure.

We applauded ourselves and
each other; never once felt
the need of a trophy.

Abandoned

My earliest memory.
Her swishing up my sister,
taking her, leaving me.

Sitting in the grass,
I watched them into the car,
flying away down the road.

The feelings set in.
Did she not see me there?
Why couldn't I go?

Tears welled up.
It was the first awareness
of what I already sensed.

Was I less?
Invisible?
Or just too much.

There are so many
tiny infractions
that lead to fear of abandonment.

She Would Sew into the Night

In my warm bed
in our old, cold farmhouse,
I listen to the ebb and flow
of Mother's sewing machine—
a sound without softness,
a rhythm of sorts, beginning slow, gaining speed,
abrupt halts, pauses and repeats.

Each seam will be arrow straight.
Darts and gathers will form the perfect fit.
Very gifted at sewing and at styling,
Her hands work and sort the patterns and fabrics
until the right combination appears.

I keep the broken harmony
And the shadowed vision of her
hunched over that old machine
with one sixty-watt bulb like a street lamp—
breaking through the vast darkness.

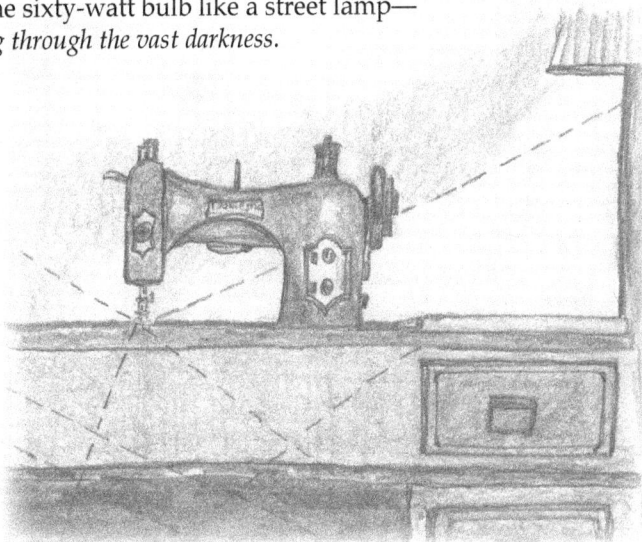

Bill Potts

James Taylor's "Walking Man Walks"
evoked a vision, even though
Bill Potts wasn't a walking man.
He was a sitting man.

Most days all summer
on his stool in front
of Bodie's Grocery . . . he sat,
gaze ever straight forward,
humming, tapping his cane
on the sidewalk,
knowing and greeting each patron,
"Good day Mis' Jane,
young ladies." His voice
had laughter in it.

Witnessing some kids
taunting him
(because he was black
or because he was blind, or both),
my father called them out
and sternly warned us:
"I better never hear of
you girls brothering Bill Potts."

His wife and children
seldom ventured into town
from their cottage
by the railroad track.

It was in Ewing proper,
still removed just enough
as not to be anyone's
true neighbor.
One son was valedictorian
soon after desegregation.

How was it
this family
lived right there,
yet we couldn't see them?

Prolonging the Inevitable

We knew nothing of it
Until the next day at school
Everyone asked, "What happened
At your house last night?"

On the night in question,
He just came in,
Sat down to watch TV,
Said not a word about it.

Looking back, I believe
I recall he had a slight grin.
He did love playing mind games
To keep us on our toes.

But this time he'd gone too far.
How could we overcome it?
No boy would venture
To our house ever again.

They came in Johnny's Chevy 409
All the way from Flemingsburg.
They were the popular boys too.
What a thrill it would have been!

Unfortunately, Daddy spotted
Them first. He didn't
Know the car and
Suspicion was his nature.

I was told by several friends,
Who thought it most humorous,
That it went down
. . . something like this.

The 409 crept along,
They didn't know the exact way
To the Williams sisters' house,
And it was a very dark night.

On Metcalf Mill Road,
Daddy came up behind them,
Noting they seemed to
Be searching and lost.

When they turned into our lane,
He drove on and quickly
Doubled back to follow them
With his headlights off.

In Daddy's defense, he thought
They were the thieves who a few
Weeks back had cleaned out
His tools stored in the barn.

The barn came before the house
And it was at that juncture
Johnny stopped his car,
Perhaps to muster courage.

Of course this confirmed
Daddy's suspicions,
And he was not one to
Let opportunity knock twice.

They said he flipped on
His headlights and
Gunned his car around the 409
Like a "bat out of hell."

He blocked any escape route.
Being frozen in place by Daddy's
Flashlight in their faces, they
Weren't going anywhere anyway.

I can imagine Daddy's surprise
As he recognized them and
Quickly figured out the situation.
Still I know he never flinched.

"What are you boys up too?'
He demanded to know.
This is the point the versions
Of the story start to vary.

Tommy said Johnny mumbled,
"We, ah, had a book Patti needs."
Johnny said Tommy kept saying,
"Nothing, ah . . . we're leaving."

"Okay. Well okay." Daddy's
Only reply, no apologies, no invitations
To stay or to go. But, he didn't
Challenge the book story either.

It was all anyone wanted
To talk about the next day.
The four boys teasing and
Being teased.

Patti and I did the unheard of:
We confronted Daddy,
Complaining that no one
Would ever date us now.

He grunted and said, "Oh, I don't think
That will happen." Something tells me
He secretly mused that perhaps
He had at least delayed the inevitable.

Rain on a Tin Roof

I really miss it sometimes,
The resonance in holy pitch.
The rhythm could be random
Or in perfect time.
It could shower upliftingly
Light and pingy, or beat down
Thunderously dramatic,
Even calmly steady and lasting.

Our house normally
Ran in extremes,
Filled with laughter and busy
Or irritable and sulky.
We weren't quiet people.
Heavy footsteps, clanking things
And hard shut doors
Meant nothing.

That first drop, sounding
Clearly on the tin, called
Us to attention and caused
Us to fall into its rhythm.
It slowed us down
And steadied our pace.
From the outside in,
We became present.

Found Courage

Most places and times
can appear glorious
if the rearward lens is angled
just so.

Is it good always to
view toward the angle
of infinite happiness?

To avoid the darker times and places,
we amp-up the light of simple joys,
creating harshness, miring the soft
security of truthfulness.

Against the background of those
gentle times of my youth,
some demons roamed among us.

As I accept my role
in holding fast to each hurt
and call out those roaming demons
with honesty and courage,
the darker parts find their place
outside my heart and are quiet.
I treat them with respect; they've
served their purposes.

The heart can prevail against
hurt and demons.
It only needs opened eyes
and found courage.

Freedom Runner

There is a part of me
that is always barefoot
and gleefully running.

Sadly, I often suppress
that runner.

I haven't always.
I could run all day
to nowhere.

Did the breezes
whistle more
secrets in my ear?

Are there new hills and meadows
now
that call?

We are all freedom runners.
The breezes continue to whistle.
Go barefoot and run in the grass.

Acknowledgments

While it isn't the nature of my husband, Larry, to engage in art and poetry, he has always encouraged and supported me in my pursuit of them. The fact that he wasn't always able to embrace the things I pursued yet still fully embraces my every effort makes his support all the more appreciated and I think admirable. So he is at the top of my long list of people I want to thank.

Next are Micki Cabaniss, my editor and publisher, and the wonderful staff at Grateful Steps. Micki recognized my poetry in its unrefined stage and patiently and steadily worked with me to grammatically correct it and challenged me to refine its constructs. Her vision and business savvy continue to create a platform for writers. I believe she approaches entrepreneurship with the benevolence and the courage to make contributing to others and to literature her primary goal. I cannot thank her enough.

Big kudos to my good friend Kathy Bott who read my work for corrections and gave me the boost I needed to move forward with it.

I have countless friends and family members who continually support and stand by me. Thanks to all of you, because, after all, you are the real poetry in my life.